YOUR BUSINESS WILL DIE, AND SO WILL YOU

PLUS 49 OTHER STORIES TO KEEP YOU GOING

PETER C. HARRIS

A QIQ PUBLICATION

CONTENTS

Health Warning	ix
Introduction	xi
Overview	xv

PART ONE
THE IDEA

1. Your life is a story - Make it a page-turner	3
2. Get bored	5
3. 'Some things in life matter, and some things don't'	7
4. Get inspired	9
5. 'Keep it simple, stupid' (KISS).	11
6. Go backwards to go forwards	13
7. There will be doubt	15
8. Learn your craft	17
9. 'A camel is a horse designed by a committee.'	19
10. Begin at the end (It's not cheating)	21
11. Determine your destiny	23
12. Learn how to fail quickly	25

PART TWO
LAUNCHING

13. Oh, you're going to need one of these	31
14. Fail to plan, plan to fail	35
15. Too many broths spoil the cook	37
16. Just do it. Then fix it as you go.	39
17. How to lose friends and alienate customers	41
18. 'If I had asked people what they wanted, they would have said a faster horse.'	43
19. Get yourself an accountant, son. You're gonna need a real good one.	45
20. 'In this world nothing can be said to be certain, except death and taxes.'	47

21. Do the right thing	49
22. 'The best marketing doesn't feel like marketing.'	51
23. When sales dip, so should you	53
24. Under-promise. Actually deliver.	55
25. Parkinson's law	57

PART THREE
SURVIVING

26. Pay yourself	61
27. Turnover is vanity. Profit is sanity. Cash is reality.	63
28. Pay up, buttercup	65
29. Show me the money	67
30. Don't reinvent the wheel	69
31. Do reinvent the wheel	71
32. Beware business awards	73
33. You're not important	75
34. Too good to be true	77
35. Payroll and pitfalls	79
36. Crash & burn	81

PART FOUR
THRIVING

37. Milk the cash cow	85
38. Diversification	87
39. Don't worry. No one is thinking about you.	89
40. Automate. Automate more.	91
41. 1% improvement a day becomes 144% in three months	95
42. Grumpy customers make a happy business	97

PART FIVE
STEP AWAY

43. Yes, step away!	101
44. Remember your goals	103
45. A 4-hour work week? Be careful what you wish for	105
46. Your job is to make yourself redundant.	107
47. If you've won the game, stop playing.	109

48. 'Your business will die and so will you'	111
49. Bonus chapter: The meaning of life	117
50. You've made it this far	119
Acknowledgments	121
Where the facts came from	123
Who you gonna call?	125
About the Author	131

Peter C Harris

First published 2025

A QiQ Publication

PO Box 76, Malmsbury, Victoria 3446, Australia

Email: hello@peterharris.info

Website: www.peterharris.info

All rights reserved. Without limiting the rights under copyright reserved above, no part of this publication may be reproduced, stored in or introduced into a database or retrieval system, or transmitted in any form or by any means (electronic, mechanical, photocopying, recording or otherwise) without the prior written permission of both the copyright owner and the publisher.

This book is published in both print and digital formats. All digital distribution rights are held by the publisher, and this work may not be copied, shared, or redistributed in any format without permission, except as permitted by the platform through which it was purchased.

Your Business Will Die and So Will You

Harris, Peter C.

ISBN 978-1-7641431-1-0

A copy of this publication has been deposited with the National Library of Australia and the State Library Victoria in accordance with legal deposit requirements.

This publication is intended for informational purposes only and does not constitute financial, legal, or professional advice. Readers should seek independent advice before making any financial decisions.

Some quotes in this book are widely shared and may have disputed authorship. Where relevant, attribution has been given or noted as uncertain. All brand names and trademarks belong to their respective owners and are used here for commentary only, without endorsement.

For Billy, my rock, and my partner in life.

And for Lucy, our cavalier, the one who reminds me that sometimes the best solution is a nap, a snack or a cuddle.

HEALTH WARNING

An estimated 20 per cent of new small businesses in Australia will fail in their first year, and up to 60 per cent of start-up businesses will not survive beyond five years of launching.[1]

Life expectancy at birth in 2021–23 was 81.1 years for males and 85.1 years for females.[2]

Conclusion: your business will die, and so will you.

Some of the stories in this book touch on failure, fear, and personal crisis. If you're going through a tough time, or you're worried about someone else, please don't go it alone. Support is available, wherever you are:

Australia

Lifeline - 13 11 14 - lifeline.org.au

Beyond Blue - 1300 22 4636 - beyondblue.org.au

Canada

Talk Suicide Canada - 1-833-456-4566 - talksuicide.ca

New Zealand

Need to Talk? - 1737 - 1737.org.nz

Lifeline - 0800 543 354 - lifeline.org.nz

United Kingdom

Samaritans - 116 123 - samaritans.org

United States

National Suicide & Crisis Lifeline - 988 - 988lifeline.org

If you're outside these countries, a web search for "mental health helpline" plus your location should help you connect with support services near you.

INTRODUCTION

Your business will inevitably reach its end, just as we all will. These messages may sound grim at first, but that's not my goal here. Instead, I want to inspire and guide you through this reality.

Think about it: if we know we're all going to kick the bucket someday, why not make the most of the time we have? Let's chase our dreams and ambitions with gusto. And as for our businesses, knowing they'll eventually fade away, shouldn't we prepare in advance to mitigate the impact of what could otherwise be a catastrophic event?

Consider these pages your source of motivation. They're filled with timeless wisdom and practical advice to keep you moving forward. At the same time, they offer cautionary foresight to help increase your chances of success and build resilience in the face of adversity.

Over 28 years in business, I kept a habit of jotting down phrases that captured something true - reminders of lessons I didn't want to forget. Many ended up in a green hardback notebook I keep close, a kind of personal ledger for things worth remembering.

Maybe you've heard them before and they've served you well, or maybe it's your first time hearing them. Or, maybe you've heard some of them so many times before, you don't know how it could possibly help. Either way, when the right words land at the right time, they can shift perspectives in a way that sticks.

I now recognise these phrases as guiding lights that have helped keep my business on course, and I'm pleased to share them, and my own insights, on the following pages. While every entrepreneur must carve their own path, and no two businesses are alike, I hope these messages resonate and help make your journey a little easier.

Having worked as a small business financial counsellor and mentor, I've witnessed firsthand the devastation that can unfold when things go wrong. With statistics showing that up to 60% of businesses fail within five years (and up to 20% within the first year alone), it's crucial to acknowledge failure as a possibility and develop strategies to mitigate its impact.

Of course, the use of the term "failure" in a landscape where success is such an uphill battle is cruel. Many admired entrepreneurs have faced premature business closures, so we must all seek to reduce the stigma surrounding business failure. Acknowledging it as a potential outcome, or indeed a likely outcome, and planning for it from the outset is a proactive approach. By all means, aspire to be the next Melanie Perkins, Richard Branson or Bill Gates, but "planning for the worst while hoping for the best" is sage advice. By welcoming the potential for success *and* the possibility of setbacks, it's my hope we can build resilient and supportive business communities.

Most importantly, the risk of failure should not stifle entrepreneurial spirit. In a world where uncertainty is the only constant, embracing risk is what makes the journey worthwhile. And, as Mark Twain aptly put it:

> *'Twenty years from now you will be more disappointed by the things you didn't do than by the ones you did do. So throw off the bowlines. Sail away from the safe harbour. Catch the trade winds in your sails.'*
>
> Mark Twain

So, as you navigate your business journey, remember: embrace uncertainty, take calculated risks, and don't let fear of failure hold you back.

OVERVIEW

There are five main stages of developing a business - and it's these five stages this book is structured around. Depending on where you are in business, only some parts might be relevant to you right now - but all will be relevant to you at some point. Think of this book as your guide, for whenever you need it You can read from cover to cover, but you can also dip into any part that interests you.

1. The idea

A business takes shape as a flicker, often sparked by reflection, boredom, or a sense of what really matters. This chapter explores how ideas form, evolve, and how simplicity (and even doubt) can lead to something purposeful.

2. Launching

Possibly the most exciting phase of a business is making it happen, and bringing the idea to life. Your business is like a candle in the wind at this stage; one gust and it may be game over. But there are always things you can do to protect it from strong winds.

3. Surviving

You've started your business, but things might be tough. You may be living payday to payday, as customers can be few and far between. The cash flow has no rhythm, and you're still sorting out the smaller details, wondering: *what can I do?*

4. Thriving

Things are looking up. You're making money, you have a steady flow of customers, and your processes are smooth. But how we make the most of it - and make things even better?

5. Stepping away

Stepping away, at some point, is inevitable. Whether for a break, a transition, or an exit, you need a plan for how your business will continue without you (or how you'll move on without it).

PART ONE
THE IDEA

'A journey of a thousand miles begins with a single step.'

Chinese proverb

CHAPTER 1
YOUR LIFE IS A STORY - MAKE IT A PAGE-TURNER

Here's the thing: you might suck at business, or you might be great at it. You might start a business, only for it to flop within a month. Like a restaurant that opens its doors one week, only to shut them the next due to a sudden crisis. But none of that really matters - because if you never start the story, you'll never know how it ends. And no matter what happens, it'll be a story worth telling, filled with lessons, memories, and maybe even a few great anecdotes. Even if everything goes wrong, you'll learn from the experience and, if you try again, you might just do things differently next time.

My point is: success and failure don't define you. Your balance sheet won't be on your headstone (unless you really want it to be!). But your stories become your legacy, carried forward by those who remember them.

And here is the twist, the thrill isn't in having all the answers; it's in figuring them out along the way.

The journey is the destination - so enjoy the ride!

CHAPTER 2
GET BORED

'If necessity is the mother of all invention, boredom is the father.'

Peter C Harris

What a great word 'procrastination' is. Even its length hints at its meaning. By the time you've pronounced all five syllables, half the day has gone.

Never before in human history have we had so many distractions to take the feeling of boredom away from us. Procrastination, most likely caused by spending a lot of time-consuming content on a mobile phone, is so commonplace you possibly can't even remember when you were last bored. Yet research has shown that it's good to be bored, because this state can help boost your creativity.[1]

In today's world, boredom can usually be generated by reducing screen time. Simply turn off the modem, the TV, and the iPad and see how long it takes for you to get bored.

Of course, another saying associated with procrastination is that the devil makes work for idle hands. Once you've freed up time to be bored, use it wisely. Think about what might inspire you to do something new.

I decided to set my business up back in 1998. It was a simpler time, and despite the internet just coming into existence, it was nowhere near the distraction it is today. Of course, there was TV and newspapers, but I was able to feel bored!

Today, 64% of the world's population use social media and the average daily usage is two hours and twenty-three minutes.[2] It's the equivalent of nearly four years of your life spent doom scrolling!

Having time to be bored and explore your own thoughts, rather than constantly consuming someone else's, allows your creative juices to flow. Why not give it a try and see for yourself?

CHAPTER 3
'SOME THINGS IN LIFE MATTER, AND SOME THINGS DON'T'

JOHN HARRIS

Life has a way of catching you off guard.

Not that long ago, I was talking with my brother - he's the executor of our late parents' will. He mentioned there was a small amount of money left in their account and he'd like to use it to help my niece and nephews attend my wedding. I was deeply moved. I sent him a note to say thank you, and his reply was simple but profound: some things in life matter, and some things don't.

That stayed with me.

In life, and in business, you'll often find yourself weighing what's truly important against what isn't. The key is having the clarity to recognise the difference - and the courage to act on it.

CHAPTER 4
GET INSPIRED

'There's no shortage of remarkable ideas, what's missing is the will to execute them.'

Seth Godin

Inspiration comes from your environment. Look around: is there a need nobody is meeting? Is it a need that others have, too? If so, it could be a business opportunity.

If you can't get inspiration from your environment, change your environment. By all means, move to another country, travel the world, and see if that generates some ideas. Alternatively, pick up a book and experience the world from a new perspective. There is nothing you can't learn, no place you can't go, if you read. And if reading is tricky for you, why not try listening to a podcast, reading an article, or watching some new content?

Break your routine.

And remember, 'if you always do what you've always done, you always get what you've always gotten.'

Multiple attributes

And, 'if you don't risk anything, you risk even more.'

Erica Jong

CHAPTER 5
'KEEP IT SIMPLE, STUPID' (KISS).
KELLY JOHNSON

KISS is a famous phrase that reminds us to keep things, well, simple.

We all have an inbuilt urge to complicate things. We mistakenly believe that complexity is a sign of intelligence and capability. The real challenge, however, is to focus on keeping things simple and making difficult things easy. When you keep things simple, they tend to be robust. There is less that can go wrong, less to maintain and less that can fail. Simplicity leads to accuracy, reliability and sustainability.

CHAPTER 6
GO BACKWARDS TO GO FORWARDS

'Learn from yesterday, live for today, hope for tomorrow.'

Often attributed to Albert Einstein

Life is rarely linear, and sometimes you have to go backwards to progress. This is equally true in business.

Sometimes, you have to revisit earlier learnings and refresh and revise.

Sometimes, it's appropriate to be inspired by the past. Invent something new by evolving something from yesteryear. Unless something is truly groundbreaking, most products and services are an evolution of a predecessor rather than something truly innovative. The iPhone would not exist without Alexander Graham Bell inventing the telephone, nor Tesla without Henry Ford inventing the first Ford motor vehicle.

CHAPTER 7
THERE WILL BE DOUBT

The only certainty in business is uncertainty. You may have the best business idea in the world, but you will still have doubts. And that's perfectly normal.

Depending on who you are and your relationship with imposter syndrome, voices in your head might work overtime, possibly causing sleepless nights, panic attacks and stress.

Don't Believe Everything You Think by Thomas Edward Kida is a great book that can help you calm your mind - and maybe stop a few sleepless nights. It dives into the cognitive errors we all make, and how to recognise and challenge them.

Personally, it helped me become more aware of when I'm letting anxiety or negative thoughts take control. By learning to pause and question those thoughts, I've been able to reduce stress and find more clarity, especially in moments of overwhelm. It's a game-changer for anyone looking to take back control of their thinking.

Mindfulness, meditation, and seeking professional support can also be useful to cope anxiety and self-doubt.

CHAPTER 8
LEARN YOUR CRAFT

There are lots of things you need to know to start, run and grow a business. First, you'll need specialist skills or knowledge - and secondly, you'll need to know how to run a business.

This book can't teach you specialist knowledge; but chances are, you probably already have skills that can be useful for creating a service or product. Maybe it's skills you inherited from a parent, a natural ability in wood carving, driving skills, or absolutely anything else people do for a living. The options really are endless. And if you are fortunate, you might call this your passion. Hone your skills, keep learning, and do your best. After all, no one will hire a bad tradesman more than once.

But you also need to learn the craft of running a business - and there are many parts of running a business, like marketing, tax, admin, and customer service. If you can't market your business to get customers, if you don't complete your tax returns, if you can't manage your staff, and if you can't look after your customers, your business will likely fail.

Thankfully, these are all skills that can be learnt, and if you don't have the time or inclination to learn them, they can be bought. This book looks at the craft of running a business. If your eyes glaze over as you read the pages, you may be more passionate about working *in* your business rather than *on* your business. And that's okay. But both are required for success. So, make sure you tick off everything you need to keep your business running well, or it might risk becoming one of the scary statistics mentioned at the start of this book.

CHAPTER 9
'A CAMEL IS A HORSE DESIGNED BY A COMMITTEE.'

SIR ALEC ISSIGONIS

As a business operator, you need a vision - a clear view of where you are heading. And unfortunately, it can't just exist in your head. You'll eventually need to document it as part of your business plan.

It will be very tempting to share your idea and get input from friends and family, and that's fine. Some may like it, some may hate it, and others will offer suggestions for improvement.

But it's important you remain true to your vision and don't let feedback dilute it, especially if you believe in it. Take negative feedback onboard. Revise your vision or, if you are so inclined, take it as an opportunity to prove someone wrong.

CHAPTER 10
BEGIN AT THE END (IT'S NOT CHEATING)

'We tend to overestimate what will happen in the next two years and underestimate what will happen in the next ten.'

Bill Gates

Once you've come up with your cornerstone idea, grow it in your head and imagine what it could become. The expression 'start with the end in mind' may help you think ahead. So think about describing your business as it may be in five or even ten years' time. And once you have this vision, you can work backwards, year by year, to create your business plan.

There is also another phrase, 'act as if'. This is attributed to the law of attraction. It essentially means that to attract something into our lives, we have to act as if we already have it. Act as though you already have your business dream and the success that goes with it.

CHAPTER 11
DETERMINE YOUR DESTINY

On one particularly wet day when I was a teenager, and I was helping my father on the family farm.

"Don't be a farmer," he told me.

He was particularly disheartened that day by how sodden the ground was, and just hard his life was at that moment in time. I can still picture the gateway where the conversation happened and the muddy footprints all around us. It was a shock to see him so vulnerable - so impacted by something as uncontrollable as the weather, especially when he and his business were so intertwined.

It was also one of the few occasions he dispensed advice to me. Whether this was the driver or an influencing factor to not become involved in agriculture, I am unsure. It did, however, give me permission, as my father's son, to pursue my own aspirations. There was no expectation to remain in this little village in rural Northamptonshire and work on the farm. It was the permission I needed, and within a year I had my first job with a bank at the tender age of 17.

We often seek permission to pursue our endeavours. But we don't need to. We have to recognise when it comes to our destiny, we are in the driving seat and the sooner we grab the steering wheel firmly with both hands, the sooner we will get to our destination. For me, that destination has been twofold: a career in financial counselling, where I help individuals and small businesses navigate debt and build a stable financial future, and running my own IT consultancy, where I guide businesses through tech challenges to optimise their operations. Both paths have taught me that, much like any journey, success requires confidence, determination, and the willingness to take control.

No one else will steer you where you want to go.

CHAPTER 12
LEARN HOW TO FAIL QUICKLY

It might sound strange, but planning for your business's failure might be the smartest move you ever make. While business books often encourage learning to fail quickly, the concept of failure itself deserves deeper reflection.

Before starting, it's crucial to define what failure looks like for you. If your business idea doesn't work out, identifying the point at which you'll pull the plug can save you from devastating consequences.

When you fail, it's not just about your idea or the product. You also need to understand the legal and financial implications. Insolvency and bankruptcy can become a reality if you don't plan your exit strategy properly. If you go bankrupt, you risk losing more than your business; personal assets like your home could be at stake, and in some cases, you may lose the right to act as a company director in the future.

Your risk tolerance plays a big role in determining when to stop. Would you be willing to lose your savings, or borrow from friends and family, or overload your credit cards to keep a business afloat? How would you feel if your business struggles and you run out of money before it turns around? You need to consider what you're willing to lose, emotionally and financially. In some cases, getting a part-time job to help support your business could buy you the time you need to make a recovery. But knowing when to stop investing is just as important as knowing when to push forward.

Much like a share trader with a 'stop loss' strategy, you should have a limit in mind for when you will cut your losses. Money is like oxygen: you only notice it when it's missing. Defining your 'stop loss' gives you the peace of mind to make tough decisions before you lose everything.

If you're wondering why businesses fail, according to CBS Insights[1]:

- 42% of startup businesses fail because there's no market need for their services or products
- 29% fail because they ran out of cash
- 23% fail because they didn't have the right team running the business
- 19% were outcompeted
- 18% fail because of pricing and cost issues
- 17% fail because of a poor product offering
- 17% fail because they lacked a business model
- 14% fail because of poor marketing
- 14% fail because they ignored their customers

In short, prepare yourself for failure, plan for the worst, and hope for the best. Understanding how businesses fail - and knowing when to stop investing - could be the difference between a failed venture and a future success. Success and failure aren't opposites - they're part of the same path. So, plan your route, know your limits, and never bet more than you're prepared to lose.

PART TWO
LAUNCHING

'What's a good idea? One that happens.'

Unknown

CHAPTER 13
OH, YOU'RE GOING TO NEED ONE OF THESE

'The two most important days in a man's life are the day he was born and the day he finds out why.'

Often attributed to Mark Twain

'Without having a goal it is difficult to score.'

Paul Arden

'Shoot for the moon. Even if you miss, you'll land among the stars.'

Commonly attributed to Les Brown

'If you don't know where you are going, you'll end up someplace else.'

Yogi Berra

There are so many quotes about goals, and this illustrates the importance of having something to strive towards. Having business goals and separate personal goals will define why you're doing what you're doing. It could ultimately define who you are as a person. When it comes to your business, is it about self-employment or escaping a job you dislike? Whatever your goal, **it should be scary and exciting at the same time.** Those are the best kinds of goals to pursue.

And to make the most of your goals, make them SMART, which stands for specific, measurable, achievable, relevant, and time-bound. This basically just means that you should be detailed in what you want to achieve, with measurable success indicators, and completing them within a certain timeline.

It's also important to consider your why: why are you pursuing your goal? A strong why can help you stay determined to meet your goal.

And finally, consider: what does success actually look like to you? Because success can look different to everybody. Personally, I feel the following quote encompasses it well:

'To laugh often and much; to win the respect of intelligent people and the affection of children; to earn the appreciation of honest critics and endure the betrayal of false friends; to appreciate beauty, to find the best in others; to leave the world a bit better, whether by a healthy child, a garden patch, or a redeemed social condition; to know even one life has breathed easier because you have lived. This is to have succeeded.'

Bessie Anderson Stanley, 1905

CHAPTER 14
FAIL TO PLAN, PLAN TO FAIL

'A goal without a plan is just a wish.'

Antoine de Saint-Exupéry

'The best business plans are straightforward documents that spell out the who, what, where, why and how much.'

Paula Nelson

'Without a plan, even the most brilliant business can get lost. You need to have goals, create milestones and have a strategy in place to set yourself up for success.'

Often attributed to Yogi Berra

You've set your goal. Fantastic. Now, how do you plan to achieve it? That's the purpose of your business plan. Now, if a business plan is something new to you, don't panic: because business plans shouldn't be complicated. It's basically your roadmap, answering the how, what, where, why, and how much questions about your business. It should be straightforward and resonate with you. Include a budget, an exit strategy, and an emergency plan for when things go wrong.

Your business plan doesn't need to be a lengthy document (unless you want it to be), but it should capture your intentions. Think of it as a tool for documenting how you'll achieve your goal, and a way to share your vision with those who might be interested, whether that's a partner, a bank, or an investor.

I remember my first business plan, back when I started my IT consultancy. It was far from perfect, but it gave me the structure I needed to get started, and made it easier to communicate my ideas to others. As I've refined my approach over the years, I've come to see just how much of a difference a clear, focused plan can make. It's not about having everything figured out - it's about having a roadmap that helps you move forward.

If you're feeling overwhelmed, don't worry. You don't have to start from scratch. Google 'sample simple business plan' for some templates. Find one that works for you!

Remember, a business plan is not static. It's a living document that you'll revisit and revise over time. It's a checklist to ensure you've considered everything needed to run your business and meet your objectives.

CHAPTER 15
TOO MANY BROTHS SPOIL THE COOK

OK, that's not quite right. The actual saying is: 'too many cooks spoil the broth', and in this context, it's about the over excitement that often comes with starting a new business.

For example, say you've bought a plot of land. The possibilities are endless: you could start a dairy herd, raise alpacas, sell eggs from your chickens, build holiday accommodation, create a studio, or plant vines to make your own wine. It's tempting to want to do it all. But the question every new business owner should ask is: can you do all of this? And if so, will you be able to do it well?

Let's take a lesson from the food industry. Have you ever seen Gordon Ramsay visit a struggling restaurant? One of the first pieces of advice he offers is to prune the menu down to a few key dishes. Why does he do this?

Well, because, with a smaller menu:

- The diner can make their choice more easily
- The waitstaff don't need to learn the intricacies of so many dishes
- The chefs can focus on quality, not quantity
- The restaurant can become known for a few signature dishes
- The restaurant can reduce the cost of supplies and food wastage

It's a lot of benefit for a relatively small change.

In business, the lesson here is that less can often be more. Focused effort, like focused dishes, allows for quality, greater brand recognition, and efficiency. By avoiding overthinking, you can stop spinning your wheels and start moving toward a more defined goal.

CHAPTER 16
JUST DO IT. THEN FIX IT AS YOU GO.

Sometimes, you have to build the plane while you fly it - or as they say in the software industry, ship it, fix it, and ship it again! The message is simple: don't wait for everything to be 100% perfect. Perfection will take years, and in the meantime, your competitors might pass you by. Instead, launch when you have something that meets your clients' needs and is ready to improve over time.

When things inevitably go wrong, treat it as an opportunity to show your commitment to resolving issues and keeping your customers happy. In the early stages, it's not about perfection - it's about adaptability and delivering value.

Dr. Meredith Belbin, an expert in team dynamics, created a framework of team roles, recognising that different people bring unique skills to the table. One of those roles is the 'completer finisher': the person who ensures projects are thoroughly completed, checking for errors and making sure every detail is accounted for. While this is an invaluable skill, it's important to remember that few things are 100% complete when they first launch.

A good team also needs 'shapers' - the action-oriented go-getters who push things forward, and 'plant' types, who bring creativity and innovative solutions. It's about balance: a successful team has both perfectionists, and those who thrive in action and innovation. When these roles work together, the whole team can move toward success, constantly adapting and improving.

CHAPTER 17
HOW TO LOSE FRIENDS AND ALIENATE CUSTOMERS

There's no place for politics or religion in a small business if you're aiming to keep a broad, neutral audience. Sharing strong views in these areas can easily alienate 50% of your clients and business partners. Whether you're a young business or an established one, it makes sense to avoid unnecessary distractions or potential conflicts. Stay neutral, avoid controversy, and steer conversations away from divisive topics whenever possible. This allows you to focus on what truly matters - delivering value to your clients and maintaining a professional environment.

Of course, some issues might feel important to you, and if advocating for something aligns with your values, it could be the right decision for your business. For example, if your brand is built around promoting sustainability or inclusivity, it makes sense to share those views. Just remember, this can be a risk, as some may fiercely agree with you, while others might disagree. It's all about finding the balance between staying true to your values, and understanding the potential impact on your customer base.

CHAPTER 18

'IF I HAD ASKED PEOPLE WHAT THEY WANTED, THEY WOULD HAVE SAID A FASTER HORSE.'

OFTEN ATTRIBUTED TO HENRY FORD

Sometimes, your customers don't know what they want until you show it to them. When creating a new product or service, you often need to trust your gut and deliver something innovative. The key is to start small - find a low-cost way to test your idea and see how it performs. Once you've proven that there's interest or demand, you can build on it.

After presenting your idea, gather feedback from your customers. This input will be invaluable in refining your offering and ensuring it meets their needs and expectations. Remember, the initial launch is just the beginning. Changes based on real-world feedback will help you shape a truly successful product or service.

CHAPTER 19
GET YOURSELF AN ACCOUNTANT, SON. YOU'RE GONNA NEED A REAL GOOD ONE.

Ah, the accountant. You definitely need one - and a good one. This person should be someone you trust, with whom you have a good relationship and feel comfortable reaching out to with any financial questions. Your relationship with your accountant can have a big impact on the success of your business.

An accountant should also guide you through selecting the right business structure, whether that's a sole trader, trust, partnership, or company. Make sure you understand the pros and cons of each.

Be cautious, though. Some accountants may recommend a complex structure of trusts and corporations that could result in higher fees for them. Don't hesitate to ask plenty of questions to fully understand their recommendations.

I've had a variety of experiences with accountants over the years. When I first lived in the UK, my brother was my accountant. He's highly talented, but I quickly learned the lesson of not mixing business with family. It's better to have a brother as just that, not as your accountant.

The relationship with your accountant should be a professional one, with clear expectations of service. It should be a commercial arrangement, not one based on family favours or casual conversations over dinner.

Useful tips on choosing and accountant may be found here - https://moneysmart.gov.au/work-and-tax/choosing-an-accountant

CHAPTER 20
'IN THIS WORLD NOTHING CAN BE SAID TO BE CERTAIN, EXCEPT DEATH AND TAXES.'

BENJAMIN FRANKLIN

Over the past few years, I've worked a few days a week on the Small Business Debt Helpline, a service designed to help businesses owners who are struggling with debt. One of the main concerns callers have is the amount they owe the taxman.

This has led me to conclude that if you can pay your taxes on time, or even before they're due, it's a clear sign your business is in a strong position. It shows you're managing cash flow effectively and are less likely to face financial crises. Setting aside money for taxes in advance can prevent nasty surprises and keeps your business on track.

Make sure to check in with your accountant regularly to stay on top of your tax obligations, including knowing exactly when payments are due and how much you'll need to set aside. Don't just wait for the end of the financial year to take action.

Another common warning sign of struggling businesses is reliance on high-interest loans. If you ever find yourself needing one, be aware that it could put both your business and, depending on your structure, your personal wealth at significant risk. High-interest loans can quickly spiral out of control, leaving you with little room to recover. Always explore alternatives and consider the long-term impact on your financial health before taking on any high-interest debt. If you do proceed, read the contract carefully, and if you have any doubts, ask someone you trust, such as a lawyer or accountant, to look it over first.

And finally, if you are falling behind, don't go quiet. Staying in contact with your tax office can make a big difference. Many people avoid the tax office out of fear, but proactive engagement, like setting up a payment plan or explaining your situation, can prevent things from escalating. Silence often triggers automated recovery processes, but communication shows goodwill and can buy you time, flexibility, and even understanding. It's far better to stay visible than to disappear.

CHAPTER 21
DO THE RIGHT THING

'Ethical behaviour is doing the right thing when no one else is watching - even when doing the wrong thing is legal.'

Often attributed to Aldo Leopold

Building a business on unethical practices will only lead to shaky foundations and significantly reduce your chances of long-term success - or a good night's sleep. In business, ignorance of the law is rarely an acceptable excuse if you commit a crime. That's why it's crucial to understand your responsibilities, whether you're a company director or a sole trader.

Nike's famous slogan 'Just Do It' was not about ignoring the rules. As Phil Knight, the co-founder of Nike, put it:

'Play by the rules, but be ferocious.'

Phil Knight

This means being aggressive in your pursuit of success, but always within the boundaries of ethical and legal standards.

It's essential to consider who you're working with and where your products or services come from. Companies have faced scrutiny over their supply chains, especially where there have been questionable ethical choices. These practices might save money in the short-term, but the long-term consequences for both the people involved and your business's reputation can be devastating. As an entrepreneur, sourcing ethically and ensuring that your suppliers share your values isn't just a nice idea - it's a responsibility.

By prioritising ethical practices, you help build a business that doesn't just succeed financially, but also leaves a positive impact on the world. And that in itself will make people want to work with you.

It's important to always do the right thing. It might be tempting to hide some financial transactions in order to reduce your tax bill, for example, but is it really worth the stress? The tax office conducts audits every year, and getting caught can result in hefty fines or even imprisonment. Not only that, but incorrect financial statements can have a huge impact on your business, especially if you plan to sell. I've seen business owners who've wanted to sell, but because much of their turnover was cash-in-hand (which wasn't reflected in their business accounts), the business didn't look great on paper, and struggled to be sold at a value reflecting its worth if everything had been recorded legitimately.

Some choices might seem like a good idea to save money now, but when it can impact you badly in the long-run, why risk it?

CHAPTER 22
'THE BEST MARKETING DOESN'T FEEL LIKE MARKETING.'

TOM FISHBURNE

Marketing often gets boiled down to one thing: selling. But it's more than that - it's about building real connections with your customers, understanding them, and adapting to what's changing in both your business and the market.

The real key to successful marketing is authenticity. Customers are smart. They can tell when you're being genuine, or when you're just trying to make a sale. Be real. Be transparent. Provide something of value. You don't need a huge budget to make an impact, just a genuine approach that speaks to your customers and their pain points. Remember: you are the solution that someone else is looking for. So market yourself as such!

If you want to learn how to create messages that resonate with your customers, check out *Made to Stick: Why Some Ideas Survive and Others Die* by Chip and Dan Heath. It offers simple, actionable advice on how to make your marketing message memorable and meaningful, focusing on clarity and connection rather than just making a sale. And if books aren't your jam, there are plenty of other articles, videos, podcasts, and other resources available for you.

CHAPTER 23
WHEN SALES DIP, SO SHOULD YOU

Fixed costs are expenses that your business must pay regardless of how many sales you make. These might include rent for your premises, subscriptions to accounting software, mobile phone bills, or the cost of computer hardware. Essentially, they don't change based on your sales.

Variable costs, on the other hand, fluctuate depending on sales. For instance, if you print and post letters, the cost of paper and postage increases with the number of letters you send out.

From my experience, it's beneficial to keep most of your costs tied to your sales. When sales are down, it's great to see your variable costs drop proportionally. This flexibility helps your business remain more adaptable in tough times.

Understanding the balance between fixed and variable costs is key to determining your breakeven point - the point at which your total sales cover all your costs. Once you surpass this point, you're no longer just breaking even; you're making a profit.

CHAPTER 24
UNDER-PROMISE.
ACTUALLY DELIVER.

The phrase 'under-promise and over-deliver' is often used in business. It suggests that it's better to set modest expectations and exceed them than to promise more than you can deliver, which leads to disappointment. However, there is a fine line between the two.

My approach is to simply deliver what you promise when you say you will. Sounds obvious, right? But it's not always. Rather than striving to impress with extra effort, focus on fulfilling your commitments.

'No surprises' is my mantra - this means I aim to meet agreed-upon requirements to the best of my ability. If for any reason I can't, I will proactively manage expectations so that no surprises arise.

As an example, I once worked with a small business owner on a tight deadline for their new website launch. Everything was going smoothly until my designer was unexpectedly delayed at a crucial time, putting the whole project in jeopardy. Instead of hoping the client wouldn't notice or scrambling to catch up at the last minute, I reached out right away to inform them of the situation. I explained the delay, reassured them that we were still working hard to meet their needs, and presented a new, realistic timeline. I also offered to provide extra support during the launch to make up for any inconvenience.

By being upfront and offering a solution, we were able to manage the situation calmly and effectively. The client appreciated the honesty and was relieved that there were no hidden surprises. In the end, the launch went ahead smoothly, and the relationship was strengthened because of the transparency.

CHAPTER 25
PARKINSON'S LAW

'Work expands so as to fill the time available for its completion.'

C. Northcote Parkinson

It's funny, isn't it? If you allow a day to complete a task, it will take a day. If you allow a week, it will take a week. Parkinson explained the concept as follows:

'It is a commonplace observation that work expands so as to fill the time available for its completion. Thus, a person of leisure can spend the entire day writing and dispatching a postcard to a friend. An hour will be spent in finding the postcard, another in hunting for spectacles, half-an-hour in a search for the address, an hour and a quarter in composition, and twenty minutes in deciding whether or not to take an umbrella when going to the pillar-box in the next street. The total effort which would occupy a busy person for three minutes all told may, in this fashion, leave another person prostrate after a day of doubt, anxiety, and toil.'

'Parkinson's Law', by C. Northcote Parkinson, in *The Economist* (1955)

This principle is essential to consider when deciding how much time to allocate to a task - whether you're doing it yourself or managing others. People tend to focus on how much time they have, rather than how much time they need to complete the task. Before scheduling or starting any task, it's crucial to first determine how much time it should realistically take. And stick to it!

PART THREE
SURVIVING

'Fall seven times, stand up eight'

Japanese proverb

CHAPTER 26
PAY YOURSELF

If you can't pay yourself, how the hell are you going to pay somebody else! Can I get an amen?

Adapted from RuPaul Charles

Do you ever watch TV shows where a couple is building their dream home? At the start, they announce their budget, and by the end of the show, without fail, they've overshot it.

Starting a business is often similar. The budget can easily get stretched, and unforeseen costs can pile up. So, how do we manage this?

The answer lies in being meticulous about budgeting - revising it as you go, preparing cash flow forecasts that you can compare to actual figures, and above all, putting on your own oxygen mask first. Pay yourself before you pay anyone else, because if your business isn't sustaining you, it's unlikely to sustain anyone else.

CHAPTER 27
TURNOVER IS VANITY. PROFIT IS SANITY. CASH IS REALITY.

Turnover is known by a number of names: sales, revenue or income. It's the money a business generates before subtracting any expenses.

Profit is the amount of money a business makes after subtracting expenses from turnover. It's the amount of money you will see at the bottom of a profit and loss statement (also known as an income statement).

Cash refers to your cash flow. This is about having money in your bank account to make payments as they are due.

A successful business doesn't just focus on turnover; it creates profit and ensures positive cash flow. Achieving this balance means your business is built for long-term sustainability.

In my early days of running my IT consultancy, I quickly realised that turnover alone wasn't enough to guarantee success. There were times when we had great sales, but cash flow was tight because I had too many staff. We hadn't properly managed payment terms or unforeseen expenses. I learned the hard way that ensuring positive cash flow -

through careful budgeting, understanding the timing of invoices, and keeping a close eye on expenses - was just as important as making sales. Once I got a handle on this, it made a huge difference in the sustainability of the business. It gave me peace of mind, allowed for growth, and made the business more resilient when times got tough.

This is something I now make sure to emphasise with every business I work with - creating the right balance between turnover, profit, and cash flow is key to staying afloat in the long run.

CHAPTER 28
PAY UP, BUTTERCUP

Pay your suppliers on time, including banks or lenders. They will be more helpful in difficult times if you have a good payment history. If you do ever need flexibility with payment, it's a good idea to discuss the challenges you're facing, negotiate alternative payment arrangements, and stick to your commitments. If you keep them happy, you'll find your suppliers are valuable allies.

Think about the suppliers you use, and make sure you share the same values and standards. It's also worth noting that the qualities you seek in your suppliers - reliability, consistency, supportiveness, and fair pricing - are the same qualities your customers will seek in you.

If you have the capacity to manage it, consider buying in bulk for products that have a longer shelf life or can be sold quickly. This can often give you a cost advantage, and having a stockpile of goods can also help ensure you never run out of popular items.

However, be mindful of perishable goods, and ensure you have the ability to sell before products go bad, to avoid wastage. Buying in bulk can be a great way to streamline costs if done wisely, and can also strengthen your relationships with suppliers by showing a commitment to long-term partnerships.

And just like with tax obligations, if you are ever unable to pay a supplier on time, the worst thing you can do is go silent. Most suppliers would rather work with you than chase you. Open communication shows respect and reliability, even in tough times. Reach out early, explain the situation honestly, and propose a realistic plan. You might be surprised how accommodating they can be, especially if you've built a good track record. A little honesty can preserve a relationship that might otherwise be lost.

CHAPTER 29
SHOW ME THE MONEY

Staying on top of the money you're owed by customers is essential for a healthy cash flow. Getting paid is the most important part of your business.

But what if you need cash before your customers pay? Don't worry: it's a common issue many business owners have, and there are a few options available to you.

The most common option is borrowing from the bank, but this is an expensive option that eats into your profits thanks to interest. And if the reason you have no cash flow is because others haven't paid you, debtor factoring can be a good option. It involves engaging another company to collect what's owed to you. The debtor factoring company will usually give you a certain percentage of the invoice value, whether your customer has paid yet or not. And either way: it's better than nothing.

Some less expensive options for increased cash flow include:

- Running credit checks on your new customers
- Taking deposits
- Taking cash on delivery and offering multiple payment options (credit cards, BPAY, PayPal, direct debit)
- Offering invoice discounting, such as a 1–2% discount if the customer pays by the due date

It's also important that you're invoicing promptly. You're not helping the situation if you're behind on your invoicing.

CHAPTER 30
DON'T REINVENT THE WHEEL

A well-known phrase in business is 'don't reinvent the wheel'. The entrepreneurs who have come before you have already laid a strong foundation in many areas, so it's worth leveraging their knowledge and experience. For example, unless creating bookkeeping software is your core business proposition, there's no need to develop your own when reliable, off-the-shelf solutions already exist.

In practice, this means taking the time to research the tools and applications already available that can help propel your business forward. Industry-standard software and established practices can save you considerable time and effort, so you don't have to reinvent the wheel. Focus on identifying tasks that are performed frequently and seek to automate them as much as possible to improve efficiency.

That said, proceed with caution when signing up for subscriptions. While there are many tools that could benefit your business, each subscription represents an ongoing fixed cost. And when you are managing a lot of subscriptions, it can easy to forget this extra cost. Be sure the value these tools provide justifies their expense, ensuring they pay for themselves in some way.

Following industry standards can significantly streamline the process of building your business. However, always keep in mind that everyone else is using the same tools, so your uniqueness will need to come from other aspects of your business.

CHAPTER 31
DO REINVENT THE WHEEL

There's nothing wrong with reinventing the wheel - especially if you can make it better. Think about how many wheels you could sell if yours is the best on the market!

And remember: don't let anyone in business tell you what you can and can't do.

CHAPTER 32
BEWARE BUSINESS AWARDS

Could it be that a business award really goes to the business that is best at completing the application form?

While winning a business award might be part of a company's strategic plan, it's important to enter such programs with a clear objective in mind. A trophy on the shelf may boost your pride, but it achieves little by itself.

In 2017, my business was fortunate enough to win an export business award. My partner and I dressed to the nines for the award ceremony, only to find that, as the event ended, the organisers had forgotten to announce our category! The plastic trophy was sent to me in the mail shortly after. And despite our initial excitement about the award, it achieved no benefit for our business.

Since then, I've become hesitant to go through the lengthy application process for any awards, realising that often, it's the best application - not necessarily the best company - that wins.

So don't worry if you haven't won a heap of awards. Anyway, the best award you can win is satisfaction from your customers!

CHAPTER 33
YOU'RE NOT IMPORTANT

Author Johnny Truant wrote a book called *The Universe Doesn't Give a Flying F**k About You*. It's free on Amazon and can be read in just 30 minutes. The book offers a powerful reminder of just how insignificant we all are in the grand scheme of things. And that can actually be really freeing.

Here is an excerpt:

'Do yourself a favour, right now, and realise two things:

1. You will keep getting older, and then you will die.

2. Everything that's ever entered your experience has lasted and will continue to last for only a brief moment in the life of the universe.

This is game time, champ. You're in. You're in, playing, right now, and the clock is ticking. So stop wondering what it all means and how you'll possibly ever do X and what people will think, and get on with your life already. Stop being a pussy and go do something amazing. Do epic shit.'

So, what's the point of this?

Life is short, and you've really got nothing to lose by giving it your best shot. So, what are you waiting for?

CHAPTER 34
TOO GOOD TO BE TRUE

There have been three occasions in my career where I was presented with opportunities that seemed too good to be true. Each involved being approached by businesses with significant resources and offers that could have been beneficial. In the end, all three fell through for different reasons.

What I've learned from these experiences is that not every opportunity is worth pursuing, and not all of them will work out. And that's actually a good thing.

One of these opportunities came from a well-known social media company while I was on holiday in 2018. I found myself trying to draft a proposal between flights, which wasn't the best use of my time when I could have been enjoying my break. It was both disappointing and exciting, but ultimately, it didn't lead anywhere.

Now, I take these opportunities with a pinch of salt. If something seems too good to be true, it probably is. It's important to give these opportunities a fair chance, but not at the expense of your existing work - or your health and well-being. When a new opportunity arises, it's worth reflecting on why you started your business in the first place and considering whether it might change the nature of your work.

And remember: not every opportunity is going to be for you. That's why it's important to pick the right ones.

CHAPTER 35
PAYROLL AND PITFALLS

It's exciting when your business is ready to employ someone. It may be at the start, or it may come later when you have too much work to do it all yourself. You may also need to buy skills for parts of the business you cannot do. While exciting, it's also important to be smart with your choices.

Some of the main lessons I've learned from being an employer are:

- Make sure you can stay on top of everything that comes with employing people, including wages, PAYG, superannuation and insurance. Get this wrong and your business is at risk
- Always pay on time (wages, super and tax). You cannot expect someone to be consistent with you if you are not consistent in paying them
- Only employ someone when you have enough work to keep them fully occupied. This includes contractors. Don't employ someone because they are

a great fit for the company, and you think you *might* get enough work over time. Get the work first, then the people to do it
- Consider not employing friends or family. It's less complicated.
- Get the best people you can afford
- Consider using Airtasker, upward.com and other similar services for smaller tasks at a cheaper price
- Be flexible if your employees need it. Employees are a company's greatest asset but a very high fixed cost. If you can work with people on a flexible basis, where their payment is related to the work done, do so

And finally, remember how you think about your work and colleagues. Author David Sawyer has sobering, but important thoughts on the topic. In RESET, he offers a sharp reminder: we often mistake workplace proximity for meaningful connection. He writes, "They wouldn't be there if they didn't have to. And neither would you."

Of course, that's not the whole story. I've worked alongside some brilliant, generous, and hilarious people over the years - people I genuinely care about and who have cared about me. But there's still something oddly freeing in David Sawyer's reminder: we're not here to be everything to everyone. We're here to do our best, show up with kindness, and not lose ourselves trying to be liked. If you're lucky enough to work with people you respect (and maybe even like), count that as a bonus, not a given.

CHAPTER 36
CRASH & BURN

Have you ever flown in a light aircraft - the kind with a single propeller and engine up front? Rarely (and thankfully), the engine can stop turning. That's where the old joke comes from: the propeller is just a big fan to keep the pilot cool - when it stops, you'll see them start sweating!

So what happens when the engine stops? An experienced pilot knows the aircraft won't simply fall from the sky. Instead, they'll follow a procedure drilled into them through training: trim the aircraft for its best glide speed and prepare for an emergency landing. Sometimes the engine will restart. Sometimes it won't, and they'll need to bring the plane down in a paddock.

The point of this analogy is that the end of a business can feel a lot like an emergency landing. Sales might stop. Your health or relationship status might change. A pandemic might hit. Costs might suddenly blow out. And in those moments, you need to assess: can this business keep flying, or do you need to prepare for a controlled exit?

It's heartbreaking to see people pour their personal savings into keeping a business airborne when it's already gliding toward the ground. Like a trained pilot, the key is to recognise the situation early and act decisively.

This chapter is a reminder that not all businesses stay in the air forever. If yours needs to come down, try to do it with care and professionalism. And just as pilots have air traffic control to guide them during an emergency, there are support systems available to help you land safely. The earlier you reach out, the more options you'll have.

See the 'Who are you going to call?' section at the end of this book for a list of free, useful resources available in your country. Don't go it alone - help is out there.

PART FOUR
THRIVING

'My mission in life is not merely to survive, but to thrive; and to do so with some passion, some compassion, some humour, and some style.'

Maya Angelou

CHAPTER 37
MILK THE CASH COW

The early years of a business can be tough. You're finding your way, the business is finding its way, and the only certainty is uncertainty. It can be really unnerving.

However, if you learn as you go, improve your business processes and are prudent with your expenses, hopefully you will, at some point, generate reasonable profits. You may be able to pay yourself a bit more, and that is *very* rewarding.

Personally, it was a game-changer when I started taking a regular amount out of my business as a wage. I set up an automatic transfer for the payments to myself, my superannuation fund and the taxman. The wage was initially low but increased gradually over time as the business grew. Getting to the point where your withdrawals are consistent and not dependent on when a major client pays simplifies everything. In the early days of a business, I recognise that this approach can be aspirational. Early days can be about juggling, paying your staff before yourself, and timing cash flow is tricky.

When a business starts generating surplus income, though, you have to tick off the various expenditures you may have considered optional in the past. If you are a sole trader, you perhaps have not been paying into a retirement pension because you didn't have to. You might consider extra insurance schemes that were not considered essential in the early years of your business (e.g. continuity insurance and professional indemnity). Do your staff need a pay raise? Do you?

There is also the nice problem of what you are going to do with the surplus income. How much of your profit needs to be reinvested into the business? Will you increase your wage? Although outside the scope of this book, investing your earnings into money-generating assets is always good insurance for the future. Automating savings is also great for saving without consciously having to think about it.

CHAPTER 38
DIVERSIFICATION

'The product that built your business may not be the one that carries it forward.'

Unknown

Just because you can meet the needs of your customers today doesn't mean you'll be able to do so tomorrow. There is a concept called the product lifecycle, and this demonstrates how the relevance of your products and services will change over time.

Predicting when a product or service is going to decline prevents your company from following suit as a result of being overly reliant on a declining market.

This is not a precise art - getting new products and services to come online when an old one is near the end of its life. There will be periods of overlap and drought.

Of course, there are also some products and services that

have an extended lifecycle, and these are easy to keep going - in theory!

Another popular expression in recent years is pivoting, which refers to the adaption of a business to meet the needs of a differing client base. Pivoting may be a trendy thing to do, but consider the risks resulting in another phrase, 'the pivot gone bad'.

It may be possible to extend the lifecycle of your product by evolving and adding new features or coming up with another business idea to implement. Either way, there are risks to manage. But the biggest risk of all is to do nothing. The world changes. Our businesses need to change with it.

CHAPTER 39
DON'T WORRY. NO ONE IS THINKING ABOUT YOU.

'When you're 20, you care what everyone thinks, when you're 40, you stop caring what everyone thinks, when you're 60, you realise no one was ever thinking about you in the first place.'

Unknown

In a world of social media platforms like Instagram and TikTok, this is a helpful reminder. We spend so much time worrying about what others think - crafting posts, chasing likes, obsessing over how we're perceived. It can send you into an anxious spiral. But really, most people are too busy thinking about themselves to worry about you.

Social media can be an important part of business. But, as my partner wisely asks, 'can you buy a cookie with that?' Likes are lovely, but they don't pay the bills.

So, ask yourself: is what you're doing actually helping your customers and growing your business? Or is it just something that makes you feel good? There's nothing wrong with a little feel-good - just make sure it's not your whole strategy.

CHAPTER 40
AUTOMATE. AUTOMATE MORE.

Automation is about doing more with less. It's the magic that makes 1 + 1 feel like 3 - or even more. It's not about cutting corners or being lazy. It's about reaching the same outcome with fewer resources, less stress, and more consistency.

Constantly reviewing how you do things - and asking if there's a better way - leads to constant improvement. A 1% improvement each day adds up to 144% in just three months. That's compounding for your time.

Take email, for example. If you're deleting the same type of email every single day, that's 10 seconds wasted daily. Over 30 years, that's more than 30 hours spent hitting 'delete'. Imagine what you could do with that time - take a long weekend, learn a new skill, write a book...

Even small changes - like unsubscribing from emails or turning off non-essential notifications - can give you back hours, days, or even weeks over the long term.

Here are some simple automations that have saved me time:

Text Expander: I use this application to quickly drop frequently-used blocks of text into emails or forms. If you find yourself typing the same thing over and over, snippets can save you serious time. I get a regular report letting me know how much time I have saved and it is usually around 2 hours a week.

Automated saving: the best way to save money is not to think about it. Set up regular, automatic transfers to savings or investment accounts so it happens without effort - or temptation.

Home automation: lights and aircon in our home switch on automatically an hour before sunset. It's minor, but it adds up - and removes one more thing from my mental checklist.

Appointment scheduling: tools like Calendly cut down on email tennis when booking meetings. It's simple, efficient, and feels professional.

Email filters and folders: set up automatic rules to sort your emails into folders or flag important ones. This way, you don't waste time sorting through your inbox. For example, create a rule to automatically flag client emails or separate personal from work-related correspondence.

Client payments: I've structured things so clients pay up-front. Online payments are automated, receipts are forwarded, and I reconcile everything weekly.

Social media scheduling: use tools like Buffer, Loomly, Canva, or Hootsuite to schedule social media posts in advance. This means you can plan and batch your content, saving time and ensuring consistent posting without having to do it in real-time every day. Many of these options have free trials, and some are free entirely under certain criteria.

Automatic backups: Set up automatic backups of your important business data, such as financial documents or client files. Google Drive, Dropbox, or an external backup service can help ensure you always have a copy of your data, reducing the risk of losing critical information.

The big takeaway? Automating the small stuff frees you up for the big stuff.

CHAPTER 41
1% IMPROVEMENT A DAY BECOMES 144% IN THREE MONTHS

I mentioned this earlier when discussing automation, and I'm bringing it up again because it matters. Constant improvement is vital. If you're not getting better, you're either standing still or sliding backwards - and neither is sustainable for a long-term business.

A 1% improvement each day doesn't just add up - it compounds. Instead of 1% + 1% + 1%, each improvement builds on the last. After 90 days, you're not just 90% better - you're around 144% better. That's the power of small, consistent action.

It's worth stepping back regularly to reflect on how you're doing things. Ask yourself:

Is there a way to do this more efficiently, more consistently, or with less effort?

In the early stages of a business, there's often a long list of things to improve - and that's okay. Triage it. Start with the quick wins, and then work on the more complex changes over time. Progress doesn't have to be immediate, but it does have to be intentional.

Now, a quick note on feedback: you might be tempted to send out surveys to your clients to find areas for improvement. But let's face it - we're all a bit surveyed out. Response rates are down, and most people don't want yet another request for their 'valuable feedback'.

Instead of relying on surveys, keep your communication channels open. Make it easy for customers to speak to you directly. You'll be surprised how often the most valuable insights come through unprompted comments or casual conversations - not formal feedback requests. And when it's genuine, it's gold.

CHAPTER 42
GRUMPY CUSTOMERS MAKE A HAPPY BUSINESS

'Every problem is a gift - without problems we would not grow.'

Anthony Robbins

It would be lovely if every customer thought you were brilliant all the time - but that's not reality. Mistakes happen. Things go wrong. What matters most is how you respond when they do.

In fact, how you handle problems can often say more about your business than how you handle success. Swift, courteous resolutions - and yes, a sincere apology - can turn a negative into an opportunity to show how much you care about getting it right.

While it might feel harsh, oddly enough, a complaint is a gift. When a customer tells you what's wrong, they're giving you a chance to improve. It's tempting to get defensive, but the better move is to thank them, fix the problem quickly, and invite them to keep being honest with you. That kind of feedback loop is invaluable.

Look at companies like Apple. They run 'bug bounty' programs, offering up to $1 million to users who discover critical security flaws. Why? Because they know the value of fixing a problem early is worth far more than the payout. A customer who tells you something is broken is doing you a favour - sometimes even saving your business from greater harm.

So rather than fearing unhappy customers, welcome them. They might just be your most loyal advocates - if you treat them well when it matters most.

PART FIVE
STEP AWAY

'I am just going outside and may be some time.'

Captain Lawrence Oates

CHAPTER 43
YES, STEP AWAY!

Did you create your business so you could live it day after day, hour after hour? I doubt it. Hopefully, you recognise there is a life outside your business - and that life is just as important, if not more so.

Stepping away isn't just a luxury. It's necessary. It's how you recharge, find perspective, and often discover new inspiration. Time away can be the spark that reignites your passion or reveals the next step forward.

As you build and grow your business, think about how you can create space to step back. You might have ambitions to run your business from anywhere - and that's great - but you still need time off. Not just remote work, but rest. That could mean taking a holiday every few weeks, planning a longer sabbatical, or eventually, handing the reins to someone else entirely.

Stepping away can take many forms: a weekend, a year, a retirement - or even something more permanent. Because, whether we like it or not, one day we'll step away for good.

We started this journey with the end in mind. That end might be a business exit . . . or your own. So, plan to step away - for a week, for a season, and ultimately, for eternity.

CHAPTER 44
REMEMBER YOUR GOALS

Revisiting your goals from time to time is not just valuable - it's essential. Life changes, and so do you. What made perfect sense two years ago might no longer fit where you are today.

Take time to reflect on whether your current goals still align with your values, priorities, and circumstances. If they've shifted, that's not a failure - that's growth. When your goals evolve, your business plan should evolve too.

Keep your goals current, relevant, and true to who you are now - not just who you were when you started.

CHAPTER 45
A 4-HOUR WORK WEEK? BE CAREFUL WHAT YOU WISH FOR

In 2007, Tim Ferriss published *The 4-Hour Work Week*. I bought the book, read it intently, and began implementing many of its strategies - automation, outsourcing, and eliminating unnecessary work and interactions.

By 2019, I'd done it. I was working just four hours a week, with a healthy income flowing from automated business operations. I'd travelled the world, enjoyed my freedom . . . and then found myself asking: what now?

The systems worked. But something was missing.

The model I'd built had ticked the wealth box, and to an extent, the health box — there was time to rest, to travel, to unplug. But other parts of me were quietly starving: I craved more social connection, emotional fulfilment, and a motivational sense of purpose. My cognitive side - that restless drive to learn, to problem-solve, to grow - was now underfed. I realised I hadn't built a life; I'd built an efficient machine. It ran beautifully - but it no longer fed all of me.

That's when I decided to learn a new skill: financial counselling. I wanted to give back - share some of what I'd learned over the past 30 years. I completed the diploma online and started working a few days a week at a local community centre. It was a new chapter, with new goals and a real sense of purpose.

Now, in 2025, I've come full circle. I'm working four days a week as a financial counsellor, and four hours a week on my business.

And once again, it's time to shake things up.

Which is why I started writing this book. My hope is that it becomes something of value to anyone interested in building not just a business, but a business that supports a life well lived.

In his 2005 Stanford commencement speech, Steve Jobs shared a practice he used for decades:

> *'For the past 33 years, I have looked in the mirror every morning and asked myself: "If today were the last day of my life, would I want to do what I am about to do today?" And whenever the answer has been no for too many days in a row, I know I need to change something.'*
>
> Steve Jobs

Success isn't about making money or working just a few hours a week - it's about building a life that's worth waking up for, with the freedom to do what you want, when you want.

CHAPTER 46
YOUR JOB IS TO MAKE YOURSELF REDUNDANT.

'The role of the CEO is to enable people to excel, help them discover their own wisdom, engage themselves entirely in their work, and accept responsibility for making change.'

Vineet Nayar

Real leadership isn't about having all the answers — it's about setting the scene so other people can find theirs. A CEO's job isn't to control everything; it's to clear the path. That means removing roadblocks, handing over the reins, and making sure the right people are having the right chats. When folks feel safe, trusted, and like they actually matter, magic happens. Not spreadsheets-and-pie-charts magic - real, human, 'I love my job' kind of magic.

CHAPTER 47
IF YOU'VE WON THE GAME, STOP PLAYING.
WILLIAM J. BERNSTEIN

Every so often, I meet clients who have taken significant financial risks later in life - using their retirement savings to open a café, or lending money or guaranteeing a loan to help a family member start a business. These aren't everyday cases, but when they do arise, they're often among the most heartbreaking. The gamble didn't pay off, and now they're facing a much tougher retirement than they ever anticipated.

I remember working with one client, a couple in their mid-60s, who had sold their family home and used a large portion of the proceeds to invest in a small café in a trendy part of town. They were drawn in by the excitement of entrepreneurship and the dream of a second act in retirement. They'd always dreamed of running a café and believed this was their chance to do something they loved. But, after a few years of operating, the café didn't generate the returns they had hoped for. The location was trendy, but not lucrative enough, and competition was fierce. Their savings were drained. The business failed, and they were left with a much tighter retirement fund than they had anticipated.

It was devastating. They now found themselves worrying about how to pay for the basics - utilities, health care, and the ever-increasing cost of living. Their dream of an idyllic retirement was quickly slipping away, replaced by the harsh reality of financial uncertainty.

Risk has its place - earlier in life, when there's still time to bounce back if things don't go as planned. But later on, it's less about chasing opportunity and more about protecting what you've worked so hard to build. If you've won the game, why keep playing and risk losing it all?

With over 75% of businesses not lasting beyond five years, the odds are stacked against you. Betting your future on those odds isn't brave - it's often devastating.

CHAPTER 48
'YOUR BUSINESS WILL DIE AND SO WILL YOU'
PETER C HARRIS

Now is the time to tackle the most morbid aspect of this book: death. It can be uncomfortable to talk about, but given the title of this book, you can't say I didn't warn you. It was, of course, an inevitability that you would end up here - just like death itself. Buckle up, but don't worry - this isn't about doom and gloom, it's about facing reality with a clear head, a bit of humour, and maybe even a plan.

Death of your business

As much as we'd like to think otherwise, all businesses will inevitably die. And at this point, I can't help but be reminded of a fitting technology analogy. When one of my computers stops working, I'm presented with two options: a graceful shutdown, or just yanking the plug out of the wall. Both lead to a shutdown - but one allows everything to wind down properly, saving files, closing programs, and minimising damage. The other? It's abrupt, messy, and often leaves things worse than they need to be.

It's the same with the closure of a business. Sometimes, circumstances will force your hand, and the shutdown will be sudden — clients vanish, debts pile up, and you're pushed into liquidation or bankruptcy. That's pulling the plug out of the wall.

But there is another way. A graceful exit. Choosing to wind things down while you're still in control - when you can honour commitments, look after your staff, pay off debts (or at least manage them), and leave with dignity intact. It's rarely easy, but it's far better than waiting until everything crashes.

In my experience, the difference between the two is often timing and mindset. Recognising when the business is no longer viable isn't failure- it's wisdom. It means you can step back, reset, and maybe start something new. On your own terms.

But even wisdom requires bandwidth. Sometimes life throws us curveballs – breakups, health issues, loss – and we simply don't have the emotional or mental capacity to tackle the situation as we'd hope. That's not weakness. That's being human. It's also the time to reach out for support. Please see the Who you gonna call? section at the end of the book for details of national support services in your country.

What if your business outlives you?

Now, here's a different kind of thought: what if your business keeps going after you're gone?

If you've built it well - with good systems, good people, and a clear vision - it might just carry on without you. Some businesses outlive their founders. That's legacy.

Take Kongō Gumi, for example - a Japanese construction company that lasted over 1,400 years, handed down through 40 generations. It specialised in building temples, but what really kept it going was structure, succession, and purpose.

Making decisions with long-term sustainability in mind - strong leadership, sound finances, and a clear roadmap - can give your business the best chance to endure. A good exit plan isn't just about you stepping away; it's about setting something up that others can carry forward. But let's keep this realistic - such outcomes are rare. Most businesses don't make it that far, and that's okay too.

And what if you're the last?

So, few businesses outlive their founder. Even fewer thrive into the next generation. If you're the last member of a family business - especially something like a farm or family-run shop that's been passed down for a few generations - closing the gate or door for the final time can feel like a personal failure. It's not.

Markets change. People change. Weather patterns change. What once worked may no longer be viable, no matter how hard you try to keep it going. Grieving the end of a family legacy is real - but so is the courage it takes to let go with dignity.

Sometimes the most loving act is not preserving the past, but releasing it, so you can step into something new. What your family built still mattered. And so will what you do next.

You're not a failure. You're the steward of the final chapter - and that takes courage too.

. . .

And then there's you

Just like with your business, there's real empowerment in preparing for your own exit. No matter how old you are: it's always good to be prepared.

Making a will isn't just for the wealthy. It's a powerful, positive step to ensure the people you care about are looked after when you're not around. It lets you:

- Choose who gets what
- Appoint someone you trust to handle your estate
- Leave specific instructions
- Make charitable donations or gifts
- And yes, shock people with your funeral playlist (bagpipes, anyone?)

And beyond a will and estate planning, consider creating a Fearless Folder - a collection of your essential documents, stored safely (ideally in a fireproof safe or digitally in the cloud), with clear instructions for those you leave behind.

Scott Pape's *The Barefoot Investor* includes a checklist to help you compile it. It's a practical gift to those you care about, and it'll bring you peace of mind knowing you've sorted the admin of your own life. Because admin is one less stress people need to deal with when they're grieving. You can download the checklist from barefootinvestor.com/resources.

Planning for your death is an act of love, control and freedom.

'Life should not be a journey to the grave with the intention of arriving safely in a pretty and well-preserved body, but rather to skid in broadside in a cloud of smoke, thoroughly used up, totally worn out, and loudly proclaiming "Wow! What a Ride!".'

Often attributed to Hunter S Thompson

CHAPTER 49
BONUS CHAPTER: THE MEANING OF LIFE

This is no big deal, just the small matter of the meaning of life. I thought you deserve something profound... or at least vaguely comforting.

Let's give it a go.

The meaning of life is simple: it's about attaining inner peace and happiness. What else is there to strive for? This is the litmus test for all your endeavours - whether in business, relationships, or personal growth.

When faced with a decision, ask yourself: what would the person I wish to become do in this situation?

Think about how your choices align with your inner peace and happiness. Prioritise contentment over the need for acceptance or approval from others.

And, importantly - never react in the heat of intense emotion. Take a step back, breathe, and respond from a place of calm.

This isn't just about business; it's about building a life where your actions are aligned with your values, where happiness and peace aren't just fleeting moments, but the core of your existence.

CHAPTER 50
YOU'VE MADE IT THIS FAR

We're nearly done, so I want to share a final thought to get you off your butt and put all these amazing words into action! Here is a definition of hell:

'On your last day on earth, the person you could have become will meet the person you became.'

Anonymous

So please, take this as a reminder to keep alive and act upon the hopes and dreams you have buried deep inside your soul. Be courageous, do what scares *and* excites you, be happy and make your life count. You're going to do wonderful things.

ACKNOWLEDGMENTS

Thank you

This book wouldn't exist without the encouragement, insight, and support of many people along the way.

To those who read early drafts, challenged ideas, or simply reminded me to keep going - thank you. Your quiet nudges and honest feedback helped shape these pages more than you know.

To everyone in the financial counselling and small business communities, your resilience, honesty, and stories are at the heart of many of these pages. I've learned so much through listening, reflecting, and having the privilege of walking alongside you, even briefly, on your journey.

WHERE THE FACTS CAME FROM

HEALTH WARNING

1. Bank of Queensland. (n.d.). The top ten reasons small businesses fail. https://www.boq.com.au/business/small-business/business-knowledge-hub/opening-a-small-business/the-top-ten-reasons-small-businesses-fail (Accessed 8 May 2025)
2. Australian Bureau of Statistics. (2023, November 8). Life expectancy. https://www.abs.gov.au/statistics/people/population/life-expectancy/latest-release (Accessed 8 May 2025)

2. GET BORED

1. Mann, S., & Cadman, R. (2014). Does being bored make us more creative? Creativity Research Journal, 26(2), 165–173. https://doi.org/10.1080/10400419.2014.901073
2. GWI. (2024). The time we spend on social media. https://www.gwi.com/ (Accessed 16 February 2025)

12. LEARN HOW TO FAIL QUICKLY

1. CB Insights. (n.d.). The top 12 reasons startups fail. https://www.cbinsights.com/research/startup-failure-reasons-top/ (Accessed 8 May 2025)

WHO YOU GONNA CALL?

When you're facing tough decisions in business - especially around money - it can be hard to know who to trust. The internet is full of advice, but not all of it is good, and some of it can do more harm than good.

The following is a list of trusted, credible organisations that offer free or low-cost support. Whether you need help with debt, guidance on mental health, or just someone to talk things through with, these services exist to help you move forward - not trap you in something worse. If your country isn't listed, try searching for government-backed business support or non-profit financial counselling services.

A word of caution

This list is not exhaustive so please note, not every website offering business advice or "debt help" has your best interests at heart. Be wary of:

- Paid debt management companies pretending to be free services

- Aggressive sales tactics pushing loans or refinancing as the only solution
- Sites that ask for upfront fees without clearly explaining what you're getting
- Stick to government-backed, non-profit, or recognised professional services wherever possible. If a site feels off, it probably is.

The goal is support, not to end up worse off than when you started.

Australia

ASIC's Moneysmart – Financial guidance: moneysmart.gov.au

Beyond Blue – NewAccess for Small Business Owners – Free mental health coaching: beyondblue.org.au

Business.gov.au – Government tools and grants: business.gov.au

National Debt Helpline – Help with personal and business debt: ndh.org.au

Rural Financial Counselling Service – Free support for regional businesses and farmers: rfcsnetwork.com.au

Small Business Debt Helpline – Free financial counselling: sbdh.org.au

Small Business Mentors – Low-cost mentoring: sbms.org.au

Canada

BDC – Business advice and funding: bdc.ca

Canada Business Network – Government business services: canada.ca/en/services/business

Credit Counselling Canada – Accredited support services: creditcounsellingcanada.ca

Futurpreneur Canada – Mentoring for new entrepreneurs: futurpreneur.ca

New Zealand

Business.govt.nz – Planning tools and support: business.govt.nz

FinCap – Financial mentoring support: fincap.org.nz

Insolvency and Trustee Service NZ – Help with business debt: insolvency.govt.nz

Regional Business Partners Network – Connects businesses with advisors and funding: regionalbusinesspartners.co.nz

United Kingdom

Business Debtline – Free advice for small businesses: businessdebtline.org

Federation of Small Businesses (FSB) – Advice and legal resources: fsb.org.uk

MentorSME – Business mentoring database: mentorsme.co.uk

Turn2Us – Support finding grants and hardship help: turn2us.org.uk

United States

America's Small Business Development Centres (SBDC's) – Local support centres: americassbdc.org

NFCC – Credit and debt counselling: nfcc.org

SCORE – Volunteer business mentoring: score.org

Small Business Administration (SBA) – Tools, loans, and recovery: sba.gov

Mental Health Supports

Running a business can take a toll on your mental health, especially when things get tough. If you're feeling overwhelmed, anxious, or just not yourself, please don't go it alone. Free, confidential help is available - no matter where you are. These services are here to listen and support you, not to judge.

Australia

Lifeline - 13 11 14 - lifeline.org.au

Beyond Blue - 1300 22 4636 - beyondblue.org.au

Canada

Talk Suicide Canada - 1-833-456-4566 - talksuicide.ca

If you're outside these countries, a web search for "mental health helpline" plus your location should help you connect with support services near you.

New Zealand

Need to Talk? - 1737 - 1737.org.nz

Lifeline - 0800 543 354 - lifeline.org.nz

United Kingdom

Samaritans - 116 123 - samaritans.org

United States

National Suicide & Crisis Lifeline - 988 - 988lifeline.org

If you're outside these countries, a web search for "mental health helpline" plus your location should help you connect with support services near you.

ABOUT THE AUTHOR

Peter C. Harris grew up on his parents' farm in Northamptonshire, England, where he experienced firsthand the unpredictable nature of small business - sometimes feast, often famine. That early exposure to risk, resilience, and resourcefulness planted the seed for a lifelong interest in how people make decisions around money and enterprise.

After 15 years in UK banking, Peter moved to Australia, where he ran his own IT consultancy for 28 years. For the past six years, he's worked as a financial counsellor, helping individuals and small business owners across Australia find clarity, rebuild confidence, and take practical steps forward when things fall apart. His work is grounded in empathy and lived experience.

In this book, Peter brings together the most important lessons he's learned - personally and professionally - about how to stay afloat in business. He hopes it offers a sense of companionship and clarity, especially if you're facing challenges that feel overwhelming. Things fall apart. Then, eventually, they don't.

He lives in regional Victoria, Australia with his husband and a small dog who believes she owns the place. He suspects she might be right.

To learn more or get in touch, visit peterharris.org.

linkedin.com/in/petercharris

www.ingramcontent.com/pod-product-compliance
Lightning Source LLC
Chambersburg PA
CBHW061208070526
44583CB00025B/3165